WITCHCRAFT SUMMON

Spiritual Warfare Prayers to Destroy the Activities of Evil Altar, Witchcraft Covens and Devils Cauldron

JOSEPH C. OKAFOR

Your Thank You Gift

As a token of gratitude for your purchase *Witchcraft Summon,*

I am pleased to present you with both the book *"Commanding*

Your Dominion" and the course *"Blueprint to Overcome*

Hatred & Rejection" as a complimentary gift.

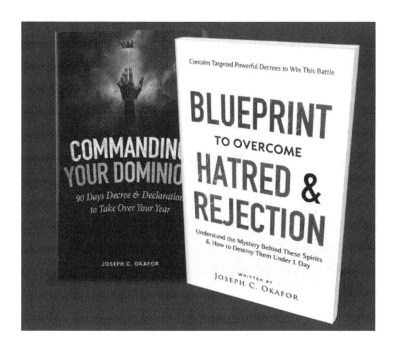

Please follow the link provided below, or enter the URL

directly into your browser ↓

<ins>cojoseph.com</ins>

TABLE OF CONTENTS

CHAPTER ONE

WHAT IS EVIL CALL

The conjuration of the spirits of the dead is known as evil summon. It is a form of necromancy. It is the capacity to summon malevolent spirits or spirits of the dead in order to magically reveal the future or affect the course of events. Its objective is to summon evil spirits, human spirits for malevolent intentions. Its purpose is to command the summoned to appear in a spiritual court. Its purpose is to summon the human spirit for a specific evil activity. Evil necromancers can summon the spirit of someone's life, marriage, or other events. They can request or demand the presence of a person's spirit or the spirits responsible for their prosperity. In an evil spiritual court of law, the spirit behind someone's marriage, business, and greatness may be summoned to answer charges. Necromancy is a heinous deed, which is why God forbids it in the Bible.

1

When thou art come into the land which the LORD thy God giveth thee, thou shalt not learn to do after the abominations of those nations. There shall not be found among you any one that maketh his son or his daughter to pass through the fire, or that useth divination, or an observer of times, or an enchanter, or a witch, Or a charmer, or a consulter with familiar spirits, or a wizard, or a necromancer. For all that do these things are an abomination unto the LORD: and because of these abominations the LORD thy God doth drive them out from before thee.

It is the same in the physical as it is in the spiritual. There are laws, practices, and traditions in the spiritual government. These demonic rulers are highly entrenched and structured in their control of men's affairs on Earth. They have the ability to influence and rule even small governments.

For we wrestle not against flesh and blood, but against

principalities, against powers, against the rulers of the

darkness of this world, against spiritual wickedness in high

places.

They intend to form a covenant with any leader from the household level, groups, and all nations around the world.

And there came one of the seven angels which had the

seven vials, and talked with me, saying unto me, Come

hither; I will shew unto thee the judgment of the great

whore that sitteth upon many waters: With whom the

kings of the earth have committed fornication, and the

inhabitants of the earth have been made drunk with the

wine of her fornication.

They utilize actual monarchs and rulers in every location to deal with anyone or group of people who oppose their long-established evil rituals, traditions, and ideas. (Colossians 2:8)

Physical authority in every city, family, or nation can be utilized to summon people to a location. We have both spiritual and physical summons.

Physical evil summoners work directly with bad spirits in a location.

And as they spake unto the people, the priests, and the captain of the temple, and the Sadducees, came upon them, Being grieved that they taught the people, and preached through Jesus the resurrection from the dead. And they laid hands on them, and put them in hold unto the next day: for it was now eventide. And it came to pass on the morrow, that their rulers, and elders, and scribes, And Annas the high priest, and Caiaphas, and John, and Alexander, and as many as were of the kindred of the high priest, were gathered together at Jerusalem. And when they had set them in the midst, they asked, By what power, or by what name, have ye done this?

Under the power of the evil spirits in that city, the physical authorities forced them to appear at a location for questioning and answering charges. The authorities of the area refer to this as a physical evil summon.

But when they had commanded them to go aside out of the council, they conferred among themselves, Saying, What shall we do to these men? for that indeed a notable miracle hath been done by them is manifest to all them that dwell in Jerusalem; and we cannot deny it. But that it spread no further among the people, let us straitly threaten them, that they speak henceforth to no man in this name. And they called them, and commanded them not to speak at all nor teach in the name of Jesus. But Peter and John answered and said unto them, Whether it be right in the sight of God to hearken unto you more than unto God, judge ye.

The evil physical council are the city's protectors of bad spirits. The disciples' message went against the established rules of the people, priests, commanders, and Sadducees. The corrupt officials in the city forbade the preaching of Christ and his resurrection. They were charged physically and summoned to court.

And Annas the high priest, and Caiaphas, and John, and Alexander, and as many as were of the kindred of the high priest, were gathered together at Jerusalem.

They were forbidden from speaking or teaching in the name of Jesus. They were physically threatened not to utter Christ's name again. All of their attempts to stop them were futile. The physical call had no effect on the daring disciples.

And they called them, and commanded them not to speak at all nor teach in the name of Jesus. So when they had further threatened them, they let them go, finding nothing how they might punish them, because of the people: for all men glorified God for that which was done.

They permitted them to continue operating physically after failing to control them with physical weapons, but they were dealt with by spiritual weapons.

And being let go, they went to their own company, and reported all that the chief priests and elders had said unto them.

They were spiritually summoned. Spiritual summoning is extremely hazardous and harmful. Evil personalities who understand how to use spiritual weapons are extremely evil. They have the ability to summon you without your knowledge. When you are determined to do the right thing but lack the courage, you have been spiritually summoned. You are spiritually summoned when you simply preach or speak without boldness. When you call out Jesus' name but receive no response, you are under spiritual summons. When you preach, pray, fast, and invoke the name of Jesus yet no signs or marvels appear, you are under spiritual summons. It had occurred to Jesus' disciples before. They were all baptized on Pentecost and talked in tongues. All of their concerns vanished; sinners were terrified in their hearts as the forty-year-old limp was healed. Three thousand folks confessed their sins. In a single sermon, another 5,000 individuals repented. They were so brazen that they dared to defy the erudite council of renowned elders. They defeated all of their physical summons. They deployed psychic weapons against them at that point. Their ideal lives had to have changed. Their spiritual guide had been summoned. They deployed psychic weapons against them at that point. Their ideal lives had to have changed. Their spiritual guide had been summoned. Their power had been summoned. They lost their confidence, and as a result of their preaching, signs and miracles vanished.

We see not our signs: there is no more any prophet: neither is there among us any that knoweth how long.

At this point, the believers of the time began to pray in order to reclaim their spiritual lost. They were brave from the start of their conversion, Holy Ghost baptism, and everyone who came into contact with them affirmed that they had been with Jesus. The gospel they were teaching produced visible results.

Now when they saw the boldness of Peter and John, and perceived that they were unlearned and ignorant men, they marvelled; and they took knowledge of them, that they had been with Jesus. And beholding the man which was healed standing with them, they could say nothing against it.

They went into prayer at this moment to fight with the evil summons and recover their losses. In their prayers, they reported the chief priests and elders to God. They petitioned God for a physical replenishment of the Holy Ghost Power. They prayed hard in humility, telling God how empty and useless they were, and God quickly reacted by releasing their prisoners kidnapped by evil men.

And being let go, they went to their own company, and reported all that the chief priests and elders had said unto them. And when they heard that, they lifted up their voice to God with one accord, and said, Lord, thou art God, which hast made heaven, and earth, and the sea, and all that in them is: who by the mouth of thy servant David hast said, Why did the heathen rage, and the people imagine vain things? The kings of the earth stood up, and the rulers were gathered together against the Lord, and against his Christ. For of a truth against thy holy child Jesus, whom thou hast anointed, both Herod, and Pontius Pilate, with the Gentiles, and the people of Israel, were gathered together, for to do whatsoever thy hand and thy counsel determined before to be done. And now, Lord, behold their threatenings: and grant unto thy servants, that with all boldness they may speak thy word, by stretching forth thine hand to heal; and that signs and wonders may be done by the name of thy holy child Jesus. And when they had prayed, the place was shaken where they were assembled together; and they were all filled with the Holy Ghost, and they spake the word of God with boldness.

They recovered all of their losses after praying. They defeated both the spiritual and physical summoners of evil, and all of their needs were met.

Neither was there any among them that lacked: for as many as were possessors of lands or houses sold them, and brought the prices of the things that were sold.

11

When your message or way of life contradicts or destroys tradition, theology, or popular opinion The physical authority of a family, city, organization, or nation will revolt, summoning you for inquiries and answers. If your lifestyles, the message reveals the foolishness of bad customs and traditions of the elders, they will refold physically first, and then spiritually second.

When I was born again many years ago, I travelled to my hometown to preach. While I was preaching, many people repented and began to preach. My family's elders summoned us for questioning. They went into wicked summons when we insisted. I recall one individual going to the chief goddess of my town, Aniagbogugu, and reporting me. We were initially unaware of the repercussions. We ignored their behaviour and never prayed against them. Later on, when some of us were supposed to marry, it became a problem. Many students were unable to complete their education. Those that finished have no excellent job or no employment at all. Things were challenging; oppressions, disease, and a variety of other problems defined our life. Some regressed, others made poor decisions, and some made poor marital and life choices. Many of us saw their growth halted, promised stars and ambitions dashed. Many rising greatnesses were assassinated, some locally, and were marked by rejection and hostility. Great prospects were suddenly closed in our faces. Many began with regret, while others died in their heinous circumstances. The remaining ones were ashamed, tired of life, living in poverty, experiencing frequent failures, and began to seek aid in the wrong places. We lost hope until we figured out how to deal with the evil summons. As soon as we began dealing with evil summoning, closed doors and missed possibilities began to reopen. Buried destinies, manipulations, and a slew of other issues began to fade. Even though we were Christians at the time, we were uninformed. Among us at the time, the last of our sisters who had only broken the shackles of late marriage married at the age of roughly 40 years.

Unbeknownst to us at the time, bad forces summoned, arrested, and detained our marriage, opportunities, child bearing, wealth, breakthroughs, successes, professions, hope, talents, memories, health, joy, and so on. Many excellent things in our life died prematurely back then, and our lives were marked by pursuing, marital failure, late marriages, troubles, and rejection everywhere we went. We lived with families, roadblocks on the verge of breakthroughs, and exam failures. Backwardness, unfathomable mistakes, repeated financial embarrassments, dissenter and dreadful disease, denial of rights, sadness, and inferiority complex. It was a major stumbling block until some of us learned the message of evil summons, evil confiscation, and spiritual armed robbers.

But as one was felling a beam, the ax head fell into the water: and he cried, and said, Alas, master! for it was borrowed. And the man of God said, Where fell it? And he shewed him the place. And he cut down a stick, and cast it in thither; and the iron did swim. Therefore said he, Take it up to thee. And he put out his hand, and took it.

A cruel evil summoner can summon your marriage in a box, cup, or other container and place it in his chamber every day to speak to it. A single broom, image, or fowl feather might reflect your destiny in a location. If you do not know how to cope with evil summon, a wicked personality living next to your room may summon your health, business, and so on into his room and whatever he says to them every morning, day, and night will be your portion. Your greatness and health can be called and given to a malevolent ghost living inside the ocean in a distant land. Your star could be in a river in Nigeria, India, or another continent while you are seeking for it in your own backyard. While you are on Earth, wicked occult summoners can place your health in the sun, moon, and stars. Your grandeur could lie in the womb of your ostensibly friend, who is sleeping with you without your knowledge. Naaman's health and cleanliness were summoned, arrested, and moved to a distant land. He was

15

in Syria, but his health was summoned and transported to another country's river. Some destines conjured by demonic spirits require a spiritual eye to discern and recover.

Now Naaman, captain of the host of the king of Syria, was a great man with his master, and honourable, because by him the LORD had given deliverance unto Syria: he was also a mighty man in valour, but he was a leper. And Elisha sent a messenger unto him, saying, Go and wash in the Jordan seven times, and thy flesh shall come again to thee, and thou shalt be clean.

Elisha assured Naaman that he didn't require medications, a deliverance program, or a protracted period of fasting. Simply go to the Jordan River and wash seven times, and thy flesh and cleanness will return to you. Those that understand how to deal with evil summoning do not have to struggle as hard. Obeying basic divine instructions can set your destiny free.

Then went he down, and dipped himself seven times in Jordan, according to the saying of the man of God: and his flesh came again like unto the flesh of a little child, and he was clean.

To some, it may be as simple as "Go thy faith hath made thee free." Go your way, and as thou hast believed, so shall it be done unto thee. Others may require you to press on him for a long time with prayers and fasting in order to touch him.

For he had healed many; insomuch that they pressed upon him for to touch him, as many as had plagues. And unclean spirits, when they saw him, fell down before him, and cried, saying, Thou art the Son of God.

Evil summoners are extremely evil. They have the ability to transport someone to very high places. They have the ability to transport someone's wealth from America to Africa.

And it came to pass on the morrow, that Balak took Balaam, and brought him up into the high places of Baal, that thence he might see the utmost part of the people.

They can summon a person or any aspect of his life for destructive intentions via enchantment and divination.

Surely there is no enchantment against Jacob, neither is there any divination against Israel: according to this time it shall be said of Jacob and of Israel, What hath God wrought!

CHAPTER TWO

SUMMON TYPES

INFORMATION SUMMONS

Through evil summon, information about a person can be gathered. When an evil summon has knowledge of a person's destiny, it might be utilized against that person. Evil summoners take communication, knowledge, and intelligence seriously. A person can be summoned by his chief village demon to examine, study, and learn everything there is to know about a person. A sacrifice can be performed to summon the main priest of a person's family or the city where he lives in order to get knowledge about a person that can be used against him now or in the future.

In that situation, the bad spirit in that location may manifest itself as a specific person in that city. If you summon the spirit in control of a location, it will emerge and communicate with you via the body of the person you will believe. To have sex in the dream, an evil spirit can be summoned to appear with your husband's or wife's face or body. In the dream, your adversary might summon your friend's body to fight you. Your adversary can also conjure a personality and pose as a buddy to you. Satan himself can be summoned to appear as an angel of light to a person in order to gain information to destroy, kill, or steal.

And no marvel; for Satan himself is transformed into an angel of light.

People who have or use a familiar spirit can even invite an evil spirit to look as a holy person.

Then said Saul unto his servants, Seek me a woman that hath a familiar spirit, that I may go to her, and inquire of her. And his servants said to him, Behold, there is a woman that hath a familiar spirit at Endor. And Saul disguised himself, and put on other raiment, and he went, and two men with him, and they came to the woman by night: and he said, I pray thee, divine unto me by the familiar spirit, and bring me him up, whom I shall name unto thee.

Summoning the dead is a pact with the devil. Everything the called spirit says may be true, but in most situations, they blend lies with the truth to confound the naive mind. They can even appear as Samuel, an angel, Christ, or even God. They have some accurate information to share since they sometimes know God's program.

Then said the woman, Whom shall I bring up unto thee? And he said, Bring me up Samuel. And when the woman saw Samuel, she cried with a loud voice: and the woman spake to Saul, saying, Why hast thou deceived me? for thou art Saul. And the king said unto her, Be not afraid: for what sawest thou? And the woman said unto Saul, I saw gods ascending out of the earth. And he said unto her, What form is he of? And she said, An old man cometh up; and he is covered with a mantle. And Saul perceived that it was Samuel, and he stooped with his face to the ground, and bowed himself.

These are the spirits who provide information about a person, a location, or an upcoming event. This is not Samuel's true personality. They do not have the ability to bring a true child of God back to life after death through evil summoning. They can only summon a familiar ghost who can transform himself into Samuel. The woman who summoned Samuel's familiar spirit was also duped and was being used to dupe others. A dead person's physical body cannot be summoned, but a familiar spirit can appear in the form of such a person.

And he cried and said, Father Abraham, have mercy on me, and send Lazarus, that he may dip the tip of his finger in water, and cool my tongue; for I am tormented in this flame. But Abraham said, Son, remember that thou in thy lifetime receivedst thy good things, and likewise Lazarus evil things: but now he is comforted, and thou art tormented. And beside all this, between us and you there is a great gulf fixed: so that they which would pass from hence to you cannot; neither can they pass to us, that would come from thence.

A familiar ghost can appear in a mask made of another person's body organs. Even in God's kingdom, God might appear to cure and deliver his children through the body of his faithful servant. When Satan deceives people, no one should be fooled.

And no marvel; for Satan himself is transformed into an angel of light. Therefore it is no great thing if his ministers also be transformed as the ministers of righteousness; whose end shall be according to their works.

The character who appeared to be Samuel was not the genuine Samuel, but rather a wicked familiar spirit in that city. The facts they provide may be correct, and the voice may sound like Samuel's, but it is an evil spirit.

And Samuel said to Saul, Why hast thou disquieted me, to bring me up? And Saul answered, I am sore distressed; for the Philistines make war against me, and God is departed from me, and answereth me no more, neither by prophets, nor by dreams: therefore I have called thee, that thou mayest make known unto me what I shall do. Then said Samuel, Wherefore then dost thou ask of me, seeing the LORD is departed from thee, and is become thine enemy? And the LORD hath done to him, as he spake by me: for the LORD hath rent the kingdom out of thine hand, and given it to thy neighbour, even to David: Because thou obeyedst not the voice of the LORD, nor executedst his fierce wrath upon Amalek, therefore hath the LORD done this thing unto thee this day. Moreover the LORD will also deliver Israel with thee into the hand of the Philistines: and to morrow shalt thou and thy sons be with me: the LORD also shall deliver the host of Israel into the hand of the Philistines. Then Saul fell straightway all along on the

24

earth, and was sore afraid, because of the words of Samuel:

and there was no strength in him; for he had eaten no

bread all the day, nor all the night.

The information provided here is not entirely correct. Samuel is in heaven and cannot be disturbed, brought up, or carried anyplace. (Luke16:26). Saul and his sons were sinners who will not be reunited with the Lord after death. All sinners go to damnation the moment they die. Saul was not invited to repentance, but was duped into believing that he and his sons would go to heaven after death. The familiar spirit duped Saul and shut the door to repentance for him and his sons. After eating his final meal by the bed of a woman with a familiar spirit, Saul died as a sinner. Saul committed suicide after eating his last supper in the wrong spot.

Then said Saul unto his armourbearer, Draw thy sword,

and thrust me through therewith; lest these uncircumcised

come and thrust me through, and abuse me. But his
armourbearer would not; for he was sore afraid. Therefore
Saul took a sword, and fell upon it.

The familiar spirit that appeared to be Samuel never delivered the message of salvation and repentance to him.

And the woman came unto Saul, and saw that he was sore
troubled, and said unto him, Behold, thine handmaid hath
obeyed thy voice, and I have put my life in my hand, and
have hearkened unto thy words which thou spakest unto
me. Now therefore, I pray thee, hearken thou also unto the
voice of thine handmaid, and let me set a morsel of bread
before thee; and eat, that thou mayest have strength, when
thou goest on thy way. But he refused, and said, I will not
eat. But his servants, together with the woman, compelled
him; and he hearkened unto their voice. So he arose from
the earth, and sat upon the bed. And the woman had a fat
calf in the house; and she hasted, and killed it, and took

flour, and kneaded it, and did bake unleavened bread thereof: And she brought it before Saul, and before his servants; and they did eat. Then they rose up, and went away that night.

The familiar spirit warned him he was a sinner but promised him of a position in heaven after death if he did not repent. There are numerous ministers with large ministries that have familiar spirits in these final days. They preach quite well, much like the imposter Samuel, but they do not mention Jesus' blood. They preach in order to persuade sinners that they will get to heaven. Ninety percent of what they preach is true, yet they fall short when it comes to eternity. They can prepare individuals to be rich on earth, to sow and reap seed, but they do not lead their members to the path of true repentance. Some of them engage in immoral behavior with their members or encourage them to do so. A familiar spirit can empower his ministers and offer them gifts, but members under such ministers would not survive. They are con artists.

Some genuine ministers who have been called by God to seek power, celebrity, and fortune have been polluted by familiar spirits. Many of them, like Samson, are unaware that the Lord has left them.

Though I speak with the tongues of men and of angels, and have not charity, I am become as sounding brass, or a tinkling cymbal. And though I have the gift of prophecy, and understand all mysteries, and all knowledge; and though I have all faith, so that I could remove mountains, and have not charity, I am nothing. And though I bestow all my goods to feed the poor, and though I give my body to be burned, and have not charity, it profiteth me nothing.

They now communicate in angelic tongues, prophesy accurately, solve all manner of insurmountable problems, and give unquantifiable charity but in familiar spirits. Pride, covetousness, greed, immorality, envy, unfaithfulness to the family, rage, and financial irresponsibility can be found in such familiar spirited clergy at times. They can communicate in tongues for an extended period of time, but then curse their members in the same dialect. They prophesy without inspiration and demonstrate powers without heart purity. Without God's love, discipline, mercy, and the fruits of the spirit, familiar spirited ministers have gifts. They can provide precise information, but they do so with familiar spirits since some sins continue to rule unabated in their life.

They can preach and prophesy well, but then practice immoral acts. They have the ability to heal, prophesy, and bless people in the church and then summon them back when they return home. Their members fear them because they can curse them and it will happen.

Come now therefore, I pray thee, curse me this people; for they are too mighty for me: peradventure I shall prevail, that we may smite them, and that I may drive them out of the land: for I wot that he whom thou blessest is blessed, and he whom thou cursest is cursed.

They are willing to give up everything to obtain information about a person. Your marriage may be arrested if they learn the date of your wedding through an evil summon. That day, you could make a huge mistake that would wreck your marriage. They use evil summon to study people's significant life dates. They strive to find out what God has spoken about a person and then waste it.

And he returned unto him, and, lo, he stood by his burnt sacrifice, he, and all the princes of Moab. And when he came to him, behold, he stood by his burnt offering, and the princes of Moab with him. And Balak said unto him, What hath the LORD spoken?

They obtain information about people's fates and waste it. Believers who do not understand how to deal with evil summoning suffer greatly in life. They may summon any wonderful thing in your life and keep it far away from you, ensuring that you suffer in life without assistance.

And a certain man was there, which had an infirmity thirty and eight years. When Jesus saw him lie, and knew that he had been now a long time in that case, he saith unto him, Wilt thou be made whole? The impotent man answered him, Sir, I have no man, when the water is troubled, to put me into the pool: but while I am coming, another steppeth down before me.

BUSINESS SUMMONS

Some people conjure the greatness and destiny of others and use them for commerce, fortune, and gain. This type of evil summoner does not kill its victims; instead, once summoned, they will take away everything great about that individual. Take their virtues, their stars, and their divinely imbued growth and possibilities. They will then implant a spirit within such a victim and send him out into the world alive to work for them. The individual will be granted a long life, and all of his endeavours on Earth will benefit others. They will suffer for the rest of their lives on Earth, but the individuals who summoned their brilliance will benefit greatly.

And it came to pass, as we went to prayer, a certain damsel possessed with a spirit of divination met us, which brought her masters much gain by soothsaying: The same followed Paul and us, and cried, saying, These men are the servants of the most high God, which shew unto us the way of salvation. And this did she many days. But Paul, being grieved, turned and said to the spirit, I command thee in the name of Jesus Christ to come out of her. And he came out the same hour. And when her masters saw that the hope of their gains was gone, they caught Paul and Silas, and drew them into the marketplace unto the rulers, And brought them to the magistrates, saying, These men, being Jews, do exceedingly trouble our city.

The deliverance of such a person has an impact on the bad persons who summoned her for business motives. Some people engage in nasty activities that waste people's brains. They sell drink and narcotics in order to ruin others. They summon such people's cravings and curse them with the bad habits of smoking, drinking, and other evil appetites. Because the release of such people has an impact on their business, they created shrines to summon those people and hold them in servitude. Such wicked people pray against their victims' deliverance and fight anyone who seeks to deliver such people.

And the same time there arose no small stir about that way. For a certain man named Demetrius, a silversmith, which made silver shrines for Diana, brought no small gain unto the craftsmen; Whom he called together with the workmen of like occupation, and said, Sirs, ye know that by this craft we have our wealth. Moreover ye see and hear, that not alone at Ephesus, but almost throughout all Asia, this Paul hath persuaded and turned away much people, saying that they be no gods, which are made with hands: So that not only this our craft is in danger to be set at nought; but also that the temple of the great goddess Diana should be despised, and her magnificence should be destroyed, whom all Asia and the world worshippeth. And when they heard these sayings, they were full of wrath, and cried out, saying, Great is Diana of the Ephesians.

You are under evil summon if you have a tough to overcome wicked habit. If you can't say no to a man or woman, you're lost in life and under a terrible summons.

And the whole city was filled with confusion: and having caught Gaius and Aristarchus, men of Macedonia, Paul's companions in travel, they rushed with one accord into the theatre. Some therefore cried one thing, and some another: for the assembly was confused; and the more part knew not wherefore they were come together.

You are under an evil summon if you cannot feel comfortable without smoking, eating a specific meal, or drinking alcohol. If you should have married but haven't yet, your marriage is under a terrible summons. If you are married but unable to conceive a child, your marriage is cursed.

If you hold a certificate but are unable to get work, your certificate is cursed. If you are constantly ill for no apparent cause, your health is under evil summon. If you have money but don't know how to spend it, your finances are under attack. If you continually take the final position and are promoted last, your destiny is cursed. You are under evil summon if you always dream and imagine yourself imprisoned up in a place. You are under an evil summon if you are constantly demoted, lose favor, and struggle before achieving achievement. You are under evil summon if you appear older than your age, feel defeated in life, feel inferior or loathed by people for no cause. You are under evil summon if you are constantly singled out for evil, attacked and persecuted alone. If you are experiencing unexplainable poverty, lack, or failures, you are under evil summon.

If I shut up heaven that there be no rain, or if I command the locusts to devour the land, or if I send pestilence among my people; If my people, which are called by my name, shall humble themselves, and pray, and seek my face, and turn from their wicked ways; then will I hear from heaven, and will forgive their sin, and will heal their land.

When a person answers to an evil summoning, he loses wonderful things.

DEATH SUMMON

Some of the demonic agents who summon their victims do not want to see their victims alive. They are enraged by their victims.

And Haman said unto king Ahasuerus, There is a certain people scattered abroad and dispersed among the people in all the provinces of thy kingdom; and their laws are diverse from all people; neither keep they the king's laws: therefore it is not for the king's profit to suffer them.

It is a great source of pain for evil summon agents to see their victims alive. They can spend any amount of money and pay any price to get rid of them.

And when Haman saw that Mordecai bowed not, nor did
him reverence, then was Haman full of wrath. And he
thought scorn to lay hands on Mordecai alone; for they
had shewed him the people of Mordecai: wherefore Haman
sought to destroy all the Jews that were throughout the
whole kingdom of Ahasuerus, even the people of Mordecai.

A person's good fortune and news can upset his adversary. They will go to any length to murder such victims. King Balak and Balaam tried everything to summon the children of Israel and murder them on the demonic altar, but they were unsuccessful. They were summoned on twenty-one altars, but they were unable to kill or curse them. (Numbers 23:1-3, 13-14, 27-30)

When they couldn't murder them, Balaam provided Balak and terrible advice to lure Moah's daughters into immorality. He tried it and was successful.

And Moses, and Eleazar the priest, and all the princes of
the congregation, went forth to meet them without the

camp. And Moses was wroth with the officers of the host, with the captains over thousands, and captains over hundreds, which came from the battle. And Moses said unto them, Have ye saved all the women alive? Behold, these caused the children of Israel, through the counsel of Balaam, to commit trespass against the LORD in the matter of Peor, and there was a plague among the congregation of the LORD. Now therefore kill every male among the little ones, and kill every woman that hath known man by lying with him. But all the women children, that have not known a man by lying with him, keep alive for yourselves.

All of the women who were employed to entice the children of Israel as a result of Balaam's advice were later murdered. Twenty-four thousands of Israel's children who survived evil summoning on 21 altars died as a result of seduction.

And Israel abode in Shittim, and the people began to commit whoredom with the daughters of Moab. And those that died in the plague were twenty and four thousand.

The information that caused the children of Israel to refuse to succumb to summon is critical. Balaam warned King Balak that as long as iniquity is not found in Jacob and perversion is not found among the children of Israel, they will remain un-summonable and unattackable. Enchantment and divination cannot be used against someone who cannot be summoned.

He hath not beheld iniquity in Jacob, neither hath he seen perverseness in Israel: the LORD his God is with him, and the shout of a king is among them. Surely there is no enchantment against Jacob, neither is there any divination against Israel: according to this time it shall be said of Jacob and of Israel, What hath God wrought!

In order to be summon-able, iniquity and perversion must be present in the victims' lives.

THINGS THAT CAN INDUCE ONE TO SUMMON A SPIRIT

Our generation is brimming with summonable candidates. Many individuals today, even some Christians, live in sin and perversion. Iniquity is a great injustice, wickedness is to turn opinions or decisions away from what is regarded right or natural, and perversion is to turn opinions or decisions away from what is considered right or natural. These two words have been utilized by the devil to turn certain Christians into a summonable community.

He hath not beheld iniquity in Jacob, neither hath he seen perverseness in Israel: the LORD his God is with him, and the shout of a king is among them.

People who are bound by immorality or perversion will become worldly. They will be interested with the ways of this world's inhabitants rather than heavenly or spiritual concerns. Some of them will readily become whoremongers, selling and buying sex and engaging in various forms of sexual immorality or idolatry. They will exhibit abnormal attachments and exhibit or display attitudes unbecoming of a normal human being in a morally wrong manner. Some will practice witchcraft, employing diabolical powers to manipulate others.

And there was great joy in that city. But there was a certain man, called Simon, which beforetime in the same city used sorcery, and bewitched the people of Samaria, giving out that himself was some great one: To whom they all gave heed, from the least to the greatest, saying, This man is the great power of God. And to him they had regard, because that of long time he had bewitched them with sorceries.

Our generation is filled with evil, cruelty, and a lack of human feelings. To be caught by iniquity or perversion is to walk by sight, to be unscriptural, carnal, and to make decisions without first consulting God. Summon-able individuals are those who live in this world but are unable to govern or control their lives. Such people lack a criterion or norm, as well as a definite principle that governs their behaviour. They study the Bible but live their lives outside of its principles. They are sinful, unfair, stained with sin at all times, and devoid of God's righteousness. To live a perverse existence is to be merciless, cruel, and pitiless. It involves being unwilling to forgive and disregarding the feelings of others. Such people also break confidence, urge others to sin, and dress immodestly in order to lure others. A pervert is cunning, subtle, and devious. He employs satanic powers to perform magic and charm people into enslavement. He is self-centred, insisting on his terrible decision, and treats his victims with no mercy.

EVIL SUMMONING ENSNAREMENTS

1. Relapse - 2 Timothy 4:10

2. Money lust - 1 Timothy 6:9-10

3. Adultery - 1 Samuel 2:12-17, 22

4. The pursuit of wealth at the expense of holiness - Deuteronomy 32:5-6,15

5. Wrongdoing - Genesis 38:6-7

6. Idol worship - Exodus 32:1-14, 19-21, 25-29, 35

7. Despising God's honest men - 2 Samuel 6:16-22

8. Strange women's love - 1 Kings 11:1-8

9. Having two lives (lying) - 2 Kings 5:20-24

10. Displaying extreme rage - 2 Chronicles 16:7-12

11. Making a deal with sinners - 2 Chronicles 20:36-37

12. Lying prophecy - Jeremiah 23:20-40

13. Rejecting knowledge - Hosea 4:6-19

14. Daniel 6:7-17 - Conspiracy

15. Divorce and remarriage - Malachi 2:11-16

16. Disobedience - (Proverbs 1:24-32).

17. Betrayal - Matthew 26:14-25

18. Holding Jesus responsible for your failures - Luke 23:39

19. False Living - Acts 5:1-11

20. Following bad practices and traditions - Colossians 2:8

CHAPTER THREE

COUNTERING THE EVIL SUMMON

E vil people all throughout the world have summoned and squandered millions of lives. More are being wasted, and many people are suffering as a result of the evil summon. Things will still go wrong if believers do not rise to challenge evil summoning. To cope with the summons of evil, we must first be certain of our salvation and relationship with Christ. We must likewise rise up in holy rage and oppose their terrible sacrifices. We must enter into prayer in order to reclaim everything we have lost. Moses was once a victim of demonic summons, but he rose in prayer to oppose them.

And Moses was very wroth, and said unto the LORD,
Respect not thou their offering: I have not taken one ass
from them, neither have I hurt one of them. And there
came out a fire from the LORD, and consumed the two
hundred and fifty men that offered incense.

Believers who have been born again have everything they need to battle with the wicked summons. If we express our anger and begin to act against evil summoning, things will turn in our favour and all of our problems will vanish. The marine powers of the Jordan summoned the iron head, which is the power behind one of the prophets' businesses or ministries. That iron head symbolized the fate of the prophet's son.

But as one was felling a beam, the axe head fell into the
water: and he cried, and said, Alas, master! for it was
borrowed.

Evil forces have summoned the true lives of many Christians. This iron head signifies the prophet's original life, genuine destiny, and the source of his son. The iron head represents God's grandeur in his life. The real object was summoned, leaving him with ineffective ordinary wood. He realized what had occurred to him and quickly began fighting. The iron was retrieved and he returned home with it. He defeated the wicked summon, and his destiny was set free.

And the man of God said, Where fell it? And he shewed him the place. And he cut down a stick, and cast it in thither; and the iron did swim. Therefore said he, Take it up to thee. And he put out his hand, and took it.

The grandeur of Naaman the captain was likewise lost to the marine powers on the Jordan River. His purity was summoned and led to the marine altars. He was a wonderful guy, an honourable captain, a national deliverance preacher, a tremendous man of valour, yet he was a leper since his original had been summoned and brought to a distant land.

Now Naaman, captain of the host of the king of Syria, was a great man with his master, and honourable, because by him the LORD had given deliverance unto Syria: he was also a mighty man in valour, but he was a leper.

Naaman set off on a trip to reclaim his glory. When he heard the gospel and obeyed it, his greatness and glory were restored. He lived a pleasant life despite the wicked summons of his day. You can also combat wicked summons.

And Elisha sent a messenger unto him, saying, Go and wash in the Jordan seven times, and thy flesh shall come again to thee, and thou shalt be clean. Then went he down, and dipped himself seven times in Jordan, according to the saying of the man of God: and his flesh came again like

unto the flesh of a little child, and he was clean.

Paul met a wonderful destined lady who had been seized by a wicked spirit. Her original destiny called her to make a lot of money for the wicked individuals around her. Paul performed a brief prayer, and her summoned destiny, her original, true-life, was restored, and she was instantly healed.

And it came to pass, as we went to prayer, a certain damsel possessed with a spirit of divination met us, which brought her masters much gain by soothsaying: The same followed Paul and us, and cried, saying, These men are the servants of the most high God, which shew unto us the way of salvation. And this did she many days. But Paul, being grieved, turned and said to the spirit, I command thee in the name of Jesus Christ to come out of her. And he came out the same hour. And when her masters saw that the hope of their gains was gone, they caught Paul and Silas, and drew them into the marketplace unto the rulers, And brought them to the magistrates, saying, These men, being Jews, do exceedingly trouble our city.

You may require seven times prayers, a seven-day program like Naaman, or just a simple prayer like in this program to bring your original back. The genuine life of a particular child was summoned, and as the life passed through his head, he cried out to his helpless father for assistance, but the guy had no idea how to deal with the awful summons. The evil summons professionals of the time continued their evil summons until midday without being challenged, and the infant died on his mother's knees.

And when the child was grown, it fell on a day, that he went out to his father to the reapers. And he said unto his father, My head, my head. And he said to a lad, Carry him to his mother. And when he had taken him, and brought him to his mother, he sat on her knees till noon, and then died. And she went up, and laid him on the bed of the man of God, and shut the door upon him, and went out.

When Elisha came into contact with the dead child's body, he dealt with the demonic call, opposed it with powerful petitions, and restored the child's life, and the mother walked back home with a living child.

Then he said to Gehazi, Gird up thy loins, and take my staff in thine hand, and go thy way: if thou meet any man, salute him not; and if any salute thee, answer him not again: and lay my staff upon the face of the child. And the mother of the child said, As the LORD liveth, and as thy soul liveth, I will not leave thee. And he arose, and followed her. And Gehazi passed on before them, and laid the staff upon the face of the child; but there was neither voice, nor hearing. Wherefore he went again to meet him, and told him, saying, The child is not awaked. And when Elisha was come into the house, behold, the child was dead, and laid upon his bed. He went in therefore, and shut the door upon them twain, and prayed unto the LORD. And he went up, and lay upon the child, and put his mouth upon his mouth, and his eyes upon his eyes, and his hands upon his hands: and he stretched himself upon the child; and the flesh of the child waxed warm. Then he returned, and walked in the house to and fro; and went up, and stretched himself upon him: and the child sneezed seven times, and the child opened his eyes. And he called Gehazi, and said, Call this Shunammite. So he called her. And when she was come in unto him, he said, Take up thy son. Then she went in, and fell at his feet, and bowed herself to the ground, and took up her son, and went out.

You may need to put in many hours of war, many nights of decree combat, or just a simple decree prayer like David to get your original back.

And one told David, saying, Ahithophel is among the conspirators with Absalom. And David said, O LORD, I pray thee, turn the counsel of Ahithophel into foolishness.

Whatever path God chooses for you, all I want is for you to stand and begin to challenge, to deal with the evil summons, and to make them bow. God gave Adam the ability to speak in the beginning, and every word he spoke was validated.

And Adam gave names to all cattle, and to the fowl of the air, and to every beast of the field; but for Adam there was not found an help meet for him.

What we say will stand, not what the devil or his agents say about us. If you pray and there is a delay, keep praying; the delay is not refusal. To cope with the demonic summons, go to whatever length. Fasting and decreeing might be added to your prayers. Be determined, and all your opponents will submit, and you will reclaim everything you have lost.

And Jacob was left alone; and there wrestled a man with him until the breaking of the day. And when he saw that he prevailed not against him, he touched the hollow of his thigh; and the hollow of Jacob's thigh was out of joint, as he wrestled with him. And he said, Let me go, for the day breaketh. And he said, I will not let thee go, except thou bless me. And he said unto him, What is thy name? And he said, Jacob. And he said, Thy name shall be called no more Jacob, but Israel: for as a prince hast thou power with God and with men, and hast prevailed.

Your condition will change as you enter battle to cope with wicked summons. If you have been reborn but discover that your life is incomplete, deal with bad summons and pray your destiny out promptly. Everything you need on Earth was created by God before you were born.

Before I formed thee in the belly I knew thee; and before thou camest forth out of the womb I sanctified thee, and I ordained thee a prophet unto the nations.

God has already provided everything you need to achieve in life, to be great, and to fulfil your destiny. They are there, waiting to be ordered to leave and come to you. God's command by his word created the entire world. Everything on Earth was created by God's decree. By God's command, all the excellent things we lost on Earth can be restored to us. All that you have lost will be recovered as you go into decree, in the powerful name of Jesus. Amen.

PRAYERS AGAINST HOUSEHOLD WICKEDNESS

1. Heavenly Father, in Jesus' name, rescue me from the clutches of domestic wickedness.

2. In the name of Jesus, I command every demonic power assigned to destroy me from my ancestral altars to fall and die.

3. In the name of Jesus, I command every angel of darkness helping my home enemies to fall and die.

4. In the name of Jesus, I break every evil agreement that is encouraging curses in my life.

5. In the name of Jesus, scatter in disgrace any evil gang-up at my place of birth that is set up against my life.

6. In the name of Jesus, let every wicked strongman of my father's house fall and die.

7. Be squandered, in the name of Jesus, every Cain spirit entrusted to waste my destiny.

8. Any force outside my family that is financing attacks on my life, be exposed to death in the name of Jesus.

9. In the name of Jesus, may every bad arrow launched into my life from my birthplace backfire.

10. In the name of Jesus, O Lord, arise in Your wrath and deliver me from domestic wickedness.

11. In the name of Jesus, every curse cast on my life by blood relatives dies immediately.

12. In the name of Jesus, I release myself from all communal bonds.

13. Any wicked force in my family that is prospering with my destiny, die in Jesus' name.

14. Heavenly Father, in the name of Jesus, rescue me totally from enemies who are extremely close to me.

15. In the name of Jesus, let any bad personality in my family who has pledged to ruin me fail miserably.

16. In the name of Jesus, let every enchantment, curse, and spell that is working against me backfire.

17. In the name of Jesus, let the Goliath of my father's house fall and die now.

18. In the name of Jesus, I command that every evil tongue that speaks against my life be hushed forever.

19. In the name of Jesus, may every devourer in my family be consumed by force.

20. In the name of Jesus, I will not submit to powers of darkness in my household.

21. In the name of Jesus, I break and loose myself from all attacks of my domestic powers.

22. In the name of Jesus, let every malicious statement spoken against me by the evil spirits of my father's house perish.

CURSE-BREAKING PRAYERS

1. In the name of Jesus, uncover and humiliate hidden curses in my life that are causing me to suffer.

2. Every secret curse in my life, your time has come and gone; die in the name of Jesus.

3. In the name of Jesus, speak destruction to every spell in my life via the blood of Jesus.

4. In the name of Jesus, I cancel every evil handwriting that is against me by the power of the name of Jesus.

5. Every stubborn curse that was placed on my life when I was a new-born, die in Jesus' name.

6. In the name of Jesus, I command the Holy Spirit to remove every hidden curse that I inherited from my parents.

7. In the name of Jesus, I divorce every curse of spiritual marriage that exists in my life.

8. Holy Ghost fire, in the name of Jesus, burn every hidden curse in my life to ashes.

9. In the name of Jesus, let every inherited curse of poverty in my life perish.

10. In the name of Jesus, let every inherited curse of untimely death in my life perish.

11. In the name of Jesus, I command that every inherited wicked covenant in my life be broken.

12. Any strongman who follows me about because of ancestral curses, fall and die in Jesus' name.

13. Any inherited curse from my parents, appointed to squander me, my life is not available, die in Jesus' name.

14. In the name of Jesus, I command that any hidden curse placed on me in my dream be removed.

15. In the name of Jesus, reveal to me all my hidden troubles and destroy them.

16. In the name of Jesus, I shatter and lose my destiny as a result of the destruction created by hidden curses.

17. In the name of Jesus, uncover every witchcraft curse that is targeting me from the dark.

18. Heavenly Father, in the name of Jesus, rescue me from every kind of hidden curses.

19. In the name of Jesus, let every strange ailment or difficulty in my life be the result of hidden curses.

20. You, the yoke of hidden curses in my life, shatter and lose your grip, in Jesus' name.

In the name of Jesus, expose every agent of hidden curses in my life to death.

CREATING FEAR IN YOUR ENEMIES WITH PRAYERS

1. Be terrified, every opponent of my destiny, wherever you are now, in the name of Jesus.
2. In the name of Jesus, Father Lord, face and defeat every enemy of my destiny.
3. Heavenly Father, in the name of Jesus, send Your terror into the hearts of all my foes.
4. Any power that attacks me with fear, get fear and die by fire in Jesus' name.
5. In the name of Jesus, speak dread into the camp of my enemies by the blood of Jesus.
6. In the name of Jesus, any power assigned to control my decisions will be consumed by fire.
7. In the name of Jesus, I challenge every Goliath in my life with the power of God's Word.

8. In the name of Jesus, let the anointing that eliminates the power of the devil fall upon me immediately.

9. In the name of Jesus, burn away every satanic barrier that stands in the way of my life.

10. In the name of Jesus, let all fighting demons that are working against my destiny be scattered by thunder.

11. In the name of Jesus, let the blood of Jesus flow into the camp of my enemies and scare them.

12. In the name of Jesus, I reject every demonic gift that has been assigned to scare me and divert my destiny.

13. In the name of Jesus, let every inherited fear that is assigned to frighten me perish by force.

14. Any wicked diversion from the devil's army working against my life, die in the name of Jesus.

15. In the name of Jesus, I command God's fire to consume every terrifying fear of the devil.

16. In the name of Jesus, I command any evil giant placed in my path to crumble and die.

17. In the name of Jesus, let every wicked angel deployed to frighten me fall and die.

18. In the name of Jesus, I command every giant in my father's home to fall and die.

19. Catch fire, every agent of irritation acting against my destiny, in the name of Jesus.

20. In the name of Jesus, strike any human altar that is burning incense against my life.

21. In the name of Jesus, let the evil altars of my father's house catch Holy Ghost fire.

22. Jesus' blood, flood into my family altars and scatter every demon, in Jesus' name.

23. In the name of Jesus, every frightening voice of the wicked hurled at me will backfire.

24. In the name of Jesus, may my appearance before all my enemies scare them with fire.

25. In the name of Jesus, I release every fear that has been implanted into my life.

26. In the name of Jesus, I cut off every evil tongue that speaks against me.

27. In the name of Jesus, arise and overshadow my life with the glory of God.

PRAYERS AGAINST THE POWERS OF WITCHCRAFT

1. In the name of Jesus, I command that every witchcraft force acting against my life be destroyed.

2. In the name of Jesus, Father Lord, I command the ministry of witchcraft to be destroyed by your might.

3. In the name of Jesus, let every instrument of witchcraft against my life catch fire.

4. In the name of Jesus, pursue witchcraft powers in my life to death.

5. In the name of Jesus, break every yoke of witchcraft in my life.

6. In the name of Jesus, I command any witch or wizard who is ministering against God's plan for my life to fail.

7. In the name of Jesus, scatter every witchcraft altar in my father's house.

8. In the name of Jesus, let the strongman of my father's home who is practicing witchcraft against me perish.

9. In the name of Jesus, Holy Ghost Fire, burn every garden of witchcraft to ashes.

10. In the name of Jesus, anointing to end witchcraft powers, fall upon me.

11. In the name of Jesus, Heavenly Father, rescue me from all witchcraft powers.

12. Any demonic personality who has entered witchcraft as a result of my influence, fail in the name of Jesus.

13. In the name of Jesus, let the bands of witchcraft that bind me be broken now.

14. In the name of Jesus, I demand that every stronghold of witchcraft be destroyed by fire.

15. In the name of Jesus, let every witchcraft hut built against me crumble.

16. In the name of Jesus, I reject any witchcraft load on my life.

17. In the name of Jesus, let every witchcraft problem assigned to me be wasted.

18. In the name of Jesus, set fire to every witchcraft marine spirit altar.

19. In the name of Jesus, let the blood of Jesus flow into every throne of witchcraft for my sake.

20. In the name of Jesus, let every stubborn witchcraft sickness in my life perish.

21. In the name of Jesus, I return every arrow of witchcraft that has been fired into my life.

22. In the name of Jesus, I command that every witchcraft judgment against my life be reversed.

23. In the name of Jesus, O Lord, free me from witchcraft curses.

PRAYERS AGAINST EVIL ASSEMBLY

1. In the name of Jesus, scatter every demonic gang gathered against my life with thunder.

2. Break any bond of witchcraft that binds me to evil individuals in the name of Jesus.

3. In the name of Jesus, I scatter every evil group rising against my destiny by the power of God.

4. In the name of Jesus, let every marine agent who is speaking against my destiny in its kingdom fail.

5. In the name of Jesus, close the mouths of evil agents in any evil gathering.

6. In the name of Jesus, let the blood of Jesus flow into any evil group and demolish its plots against me.

7. In the name of Jesus, scatter any evil throng gathered against me.

8. In the name of Jesus, let the army of darkness assigned to waste me be wasted.

9. In the name of Jesus, let the Holy Spirit's hand blow and disperse my foes.

10. In the name of Jesus, let every stronghold of witchcraft against my life crumble.

11. Any nefarious plan against my destiny, fail miserably by fire, in Jesus' name.

12. In the name of Jesus, let any evil weapon gathering demons against my life catch fire.

13. In the name of Jesus, end the ministry of evil gang-up in my life.

1. 14 In the name of Jesus, the personality that is rallying wicked people against me will fail.

14. In the name of Jesus, let all my enemies be defeated in their gathering places.

15. In the name of Jesus, I destroy every satanic gathering by the anointing of the Holy Spirit.

16. In the name of Jesus, O Lord, send Your angels to combat every evil activity in the nation.

2. In the name of Jesus, I will put to shame the ancestral powers that have assembled against me.

3. 19. Blood of Jesus, rescue me now from every evil gathering, in Jesus' name.

21. In the name of Jesus, O Lord, spare my life from every marine gang-up against me.

22. In the name of Jesus, I command that any curse of the enemy in my life be burned by fire.

23. In the name of Jesus, cancel every bad pronouncement in any evil meeting.

24. In the name of Jesus, I reject any evil agreement formed against me.

25. Lord Jesus, arise and shame my enemies in Jesus' name.

PRAYERS AGAINST RESILIENT ADVERSARIES

1. In the name of Jesus, let every obstinate foe of my breakthrough perish.

2. O Lord, deliver me from the obstinate enemy who refuses to let me go, in Jesus' name.

3. Holy Spirit, empower me to shame my obstinate opponents in Jesus' name.

4. In the name of Jesus, let every marine problem in my life perish.

5. In the name of Jesus, I destroy every enemy on the battlefield against me by the power of God.

6. In the name of Jesus, may every sickness destined to destroy me be consumed by fire.

7. Heavenly warriors, box all my foes to death in Jesus' name.

8. In the name of Jesus, I begin to move out of the prison of demonic altars.

9. In the name of Jesus, Father Lord, use the weapons of signs and wonders to save me from the great enemy.

10. In the name of Jesus, I command the enemy's spiritual aggression against me to cease.

11. In the name of Jesus, O Lord, grant me Your anointing to defeat the enemies of my spirit.

12. In the name of Jesus, I command you to close every evil door in my life.

13. Disgrace the altars of evil that struggle against my soul, in Jesus' name.

14. Any power that proclaims my name for evil, shut your lips and die in the name of Jesus.

15. In the name of Jesus, may the wicked fire that is burning against me be extinguished by force.

16. In the name of Jesus, I command that every demonic resurgence in my life be put to death.

17. Any bad leg ready to enter my life, turn back, walk back to your source, in Jesus' name.

18. In the name of Jesus, shame every opponent of my promotion.

19. In the name of Jesus, I disband every army of the wicked collected against me.

20. Every obstinate foe of my destiny, fall and die in the name of Jesus.

21. In the name of Jesus, I break and loose my destiny from every enemy of my spirit.

22. In the name of Jesus, return any bad arrows that have been launched into my life.

23. In the name of Jesus, may every good thing that my adversaries have buried against me be exhumed by thunder.

24. Holy Spirit, energise me to demolish all my enemies in Jesus' name.

25. In the name of Jesus, I close my opponents' mouths by the power in his blood.

OPEN DOORS PRAYERS

1. Father, Lord, open divine doors that will make me big in Jesus' name.

2. Lord Jesus, arise and open tremendous doors for me today in Jesus' name.

3. Heavenly Father, in the name of Jesus, break every yoke of poverty in my life.

4. Disgrace every enemy of my open doors, in the name of Jesus.

5. In the name of Jesus, catch any demonic trap assigned to catch me.

6. In the name of Jesus, let every foe of my glorious harvest fall and perish.

7. In the name of Jesus, I command that any Jericho wall that stands in the way of my breakthrough be destroyed by fire.

8. In the name of Jesus, let my heavens open by fire and my miracle show.

9. In the name of Jesus, let every obstacle that seeks to close the doors to my blessings be consumed by fire.

10. In the name of Jesus, Father Lord, may my life attract heavenly favor.

11. Miracle gates, open for my cause in every city of the world, in Jesus' name.

12. Every serpent that stands in my way, I will chop off your head with fire in the name of Jesus.

13. In the name of Jesus, break every appointment with poverty in my life with fire.

14. Any evil agent standing in my way to grandeur, fall and perish in Jesus' name.

15. In the name of Jesus, let the armies of heaven drive the doors of greatness open.

16. In the name of Jesus, let every satanic barrier that stands in my way of prosperity crumble like thunder.

17. In the name of Jesus, make every apparent and invisible impediment to my life emerge.

18. In the name of Jesus, Holy Spirit fire, burn every satanic sacrifice against me to ashes.

19. In the name of Jesus, open huge doors for me by the blood of Jesus.

20. In the name of Jesus, I command that any evil spying against my breakthrough be removed.

21. In the name of Jesus, let the might of God destroy every evil weapon that stands in my way to God.

22. In the name of Jesus, I command that any bad barrier to my promotion be roasted by fire.

23. In the name of Jesus, let every difficulty that seeks to end my path with God perish.

24. In the name of Jesus, let every evil plot against my life perish.

25. Clear away every veil of darkness that has enslaved me, in the name of Jesus.

26. Come down, my suspended marvels, in the name of Jesus.

Your Thank You Gift

As a token of gratitude for your purchase *Witchcraft Summon,* I am pleased to present you with both the book *"Commanding Your Dominion"* and the course *"Blueprint to Overcome Hatred & Rejection" as a complimentary gift.*

Please follow the link provided below, or enter the URL directly into your browser ↓

cojoseph.com

Made in United States
Troutdale, OR
01/16/2024

16973821R00046